LEGENDS OF WARFARE

NAVAL

PT Boats

The US Navy's Fast Attack Patrol Torpedo Boats in World War II

DAVID DOYLE

SCHIFFER MILITARY

4880 Lower Valley Road   Atglen, PA 19310

Designed by Justin Watkinson
Type set in Impact/Minion Pro/Univers LT Std

ISBN: 978-0-7643-5666-7
Printed in China

Published by Schiffer Publishing, Ltd.
4880 Lower Valley Road
Atglen, PA 19310
Phone: (610) 593-1777; Fax: (610) 593-2002
E-mail: Info@schifferbooks.com
www.schifferbooks.com

For our complete selection of fine books on this and related subjects, please visit our website at www.schifferbooks.com. You may also write for a free catalog.

Schiffer Publishing's titles are available at special discounts for bulk purchases for sales promotions or premiums. Special editions, including personalized covers, corporate imprints, and excerpts, can be created in large quantities for special needs. For more information, contact the publisher.

We are always looking for people to write books on new and related subjects. If you have an idea for a book, please contact us at proposals@schifferbooks.com.

Acknowledgments

As with all of my projects, this book would not have been possible without the generous help of many friends. Instrumental to the completion of this book were Tom Kailbourn; Tracy White; Sean Hert; Scott Taylor; David Jackson; the staff and volunteers at PT Boats Inc., Battleship Cove, Save the PT Boat Inc., and the National Museum of the Pacific War; and Robert Hanshew, with the Naval History and Heritage Command, and the late Jim Alexander. Most importantly, I am blessed to have the help and support of my wife, Denise, for which I am eternally grateful.

All photos from the collection of PT Boats Inc., unless otherwise noted.

Contents

	Introduction	004
CHAPTER 1	**Elco PT-10 through PT-19**	010
CHAPTER 2	**Elco 77-Foot Boats**	018
CHAPTER 3	**Higgins 78-Foot Boats**	034
CHAPTER 4	**Huckins and Canadian Powerboats**	086
CHAPTER 5	**Elco 80-Foot Boats**	091

Introduction

The fast, heavily armed American PT (**P**atrol **T**orpedo) boat rose to considerable fame in World War II, largely due to the heroics of their crews, a fame that was further fueled by the movie *They Were Expendable* as well as by Lt. (later president) John F. Kennedy's loss of PT-109. Work on creating these iconic vessels began in the 1930s, well before the US entry into World War II.

Public fascination with these vessels has also led to numerous myths being spread. Foremost of those is that they were built of plywood (in fact, most were built of mahogany planks, and one of aluminum), and that they were powered by the same engine as the North American P-51 Mustang and Supermarine Spitfire, the Packard (Rolls-Royce) Merlin. While the boats were powered by Packard engines, only one had Merlin power; all the rest were powered by Packard Marine engines, having nothing at all in common with the Merlin.

The US Navy's famed PT boats of the World War II era were the result of a design competition initiated in 1938. The first four boats, PT-1 through PT-4, were designed by George Crouch and built by Miami Shipbuilding and Fisher Boat Works. Three further boats were built by Higgins Industries: PT-5 and PT-6 were built to a Sparkman and Stephens design, while the third boat, PT-6 "Prime," incorporated some of Andrew Jackson Higgins' own design changes. Later in the year, Higgins built a fourth boat at their own expense and of their own design. This was dubbed PT-70.

Navy designers laid out PT-7 and PT-8, which were built at the Philadelphia Navy Yard. Testing of all these boats revealed room for improvement, and a further round of experimental boats was in order.

With the encouragement of the Franklin D. Roosevelt administration, Henry Supthen, vice president of the Electric Launch Corporation (Elco), along with his designers Irwin Chase, Bill Fleming, and Glenville Tremaine, traveled to England in February 1939. During a visit to the British Power Boat Company, Supthen bought the PV-70 Motor Torpedo Boat, designed by Hubert Scott-Paine, as well as a license to produce torpedo boats to Scott-Paine's design. PV-70 was powered by Rolls-Royce Merlins, and after its sale by Elco to the Navy, which designated it the PT-9 boat, this became the *only* Merlin-powered PT boat owned by the US Navy, although it was subsequently reengined with Packards. This boat would serve as a prototype for Elco's 1939-contracted PT-10- through PT-19-class boats, although these boats, like all subsequent US PTs, were powered by Packard Marine engines.

Frank Pembroke Huckins of Florida's Huckins Yacht Corporation also offered a design to the Navy. An agreement was reached, and Huckins produced the PT-69.

In March 1941, a competition among designs, dubbed the Plywood Derby, was held. This included a heavy-weather run from Key West, Florida, to New York. This test revealed deficiencies in all the designs, and further comparative service tests were held off New London, Connecticut, in July 1941, and yet another in August 1941. In all these tests the Elco boats were found to pound heavily, and all but the Navy Yard and Higgins 80-foot PT-6 boat exhibited structural failure.

Following these tests, the Navy Board of Inspection and Survey arrived at the following recommendations:

That the Packard power plant, having been found highly satisfactory, be adopted as standard for future construction.
That the ordnance installation of future motor torpedo boats consist of two torpedo tubes, machine guns, and depth charges.

PT-1 was built by Fogal Boat Yard Inc., of Miami, Florida, which began construction in July 1938 but did not complete the vessel until November 1941, too late for the Navy follow-on competition. Adjacent to the torpedo tube can be seen one of two massive mufflers provided for the engines. One month after delivery, the boat was reclassified as small boat C-6083.

That the Huckins 78-foot (PT-69) design be considered acceptable for immediate construction.

That the Higgins 80-foot (PT-6) design, suitably reduced in size to carry such ordnance loads as are required by our Navy, be considered acceptable for immediate construction.

That the Elco 77-foot design be considered acceptable for future construction, provided that changes in the lines are made to reduce the tendency to pound in a seaway, and the structure be strengthened in a manner acceptable to the Bureau of Ships.

That the Philadelphia 81-foot boat (PT-8) be stripped of excess weight and be reengined with three Packard engines.

The board also published its recommendations, which were the following:

The Packard engines were the engines of choice.

The Huckins 72-foot (PT-69) and a reduced Higgins 81-foot (PT-6) design were to be placed into production.

Following an October 1941 BuShips conference and its new set of Navy design requirements, which included room to support four 21-inch (53 cm) torpedoes and an upper length restriction of 82 feet, the next two orders for prewar PT boats (PT-71 through PT-102) were awarded to Higgins and Huckins.

Even though the Elco 77-footers posted the fastest speeds, all seven Elcos suffered from structural damage and severe pounding, causing the Board of Inspection and Survey to recommend a redesign to correct these deficiencies. Elco competed for the PT-71 to PT-102 contract but did not win due to their higher unit price. After the start of the war, Elco significantly revised their unit cost and then received the next PT boat order after Higgins and Huckins. This was to be their new Elco 80-foot design.

PT-2 was also built by Fogal Boat Yard. Delivery of the two George Crouch–designed boats was delayed two years due to problems obtaining the 1,200-horsepower Vimalert engines. Like its sister, it was reclassified as a small boat on Christmas Eve 1941.

Also designed by George Crouch but built by the Fisher Boat Works of Detroit, PT-3 and PT-4 were 58-foot boats with rearward-firing torpedo tubes. These boats ended their military career being used by the Royal Canadian Air Force as rescue boats.

New Orleans–based Higgins Industries, Inc., built two 81-foot boats based on designs by Sparkman & Stephens, famed naval architects; those boats were PT-5 and PT-6. The Sparkman & Stephens–designed PT-6 was completed in August 1940 and subsequently was sold to Finland. A second PT-6, shown here, was then built to Higgins's own design and was completed in February 1941.

Two experimental 81-foot patrol-torpedo boats, PT-7 and PT-8, were built at the Philadelphia Navy Yard. PT-7 is shown here under construction on October 4, 1940. This boat had a wooden hull, while its sister, PT-8, had an all-aluminum hull. A key feature of PT-7 was the rounded upper corners of the hull. To the port side of the boat is a charthouse assembly, which appears to be the one used on PT-8.
National Archives

The starboard side of PT-7 is viewed from a perspective more to the aft during construction on October 4, 1940. The boat was launched on October 30, 1940. Completed on February 21, 1941, it was transferred to the Royal Navy that April; the British then transferred it to the Royal Canadian Air Force, which used it as a rescue boat. After being returned to the United States in 1945, it was used as a target boat and was sunk in April of that same year. *National Archives*

PT-8, with its all-aluminum hull, is shown under construction at the Philadelphia Navy Yard on July 11, 1940. Work commenced on the boat in late December 1939, and it was launched on October 29, 1940. *National Archives*

Commissioned as PT-8 on February 8, 1941, the boat, shown here at speed, was redesignated YP-110 the following October and served as a district patrol craft. The boat survived and, as of recently, is in private hands.

This unmarked PT boat firing a torpedo during 1939 US Navy trials was in fact not built in the United States. Rather, it was built in Britain by Scott-Paine, which designated the craft Motor Torpedo Boat PV-70. The private-venture boat was purchased for $300,000 by Elco in March 1939, which also obtained a license to produce boats based on the PV-70 design.

CHAPTER 1
Elco PT-10 through PT-19

After the successful demonstration of the Merlin-powered PT-9, designed and built by Scott-Paine, the Navy opted to order near duplicates from Scott-Paine's US licensee, Elco. On December 7, 1939, the Navy awarded the Bayonne-based firm a contract for eleven motor torpedo boats, numbered PT-10 through PT-20. The estimated value of the contract for these vessels was $5,000,000.

These boats were to be the first true production class of US motor torpedo boats. At 70 feet long, the Elco boats differed from their Scott-Paine pattern (PT-9) in being powered by three Packard 4M-2500 1,200-horsepower V-12 marine engines, rather than Rolls-Royce Merlins, and in having a redesigned cabin and enlarged pilothouse.

Construction of the boats began in January 1940 and featured a keel made of hand-hewn Alaskan spruce, and a stem of American oak. The hull frames, along with the hull planking, were African mahogany. The hull and deck were constructed of double layers of planking laid diagonally. Between the layers was airplane fabric that was impregnated with marine glue. This layered construction provided extra strength and watertightness.

Armament of the boats consisted of four 18-inch torpedo tubes, and a pair of Dutch-made Dewandre hydraulically powered twin .50-caliber machine gun turrets with Plexiglas canopies.

The center engine was direct drive, whereas each side engine drove its propeller through a V-drive. At top speed, the trio was capable of propelling the boats at speeds up to 39 knots. Fuel was 100-octane aviation gasoline, which typically was consumed at a rate of 150 gallons per hour, per engine.

Delivery of the boats began in November 1940, with PT-10 being placed in service on November 7, and PT-11 and PT-12 being delivered on November 12 and 14, respectively. Placed in service with Motor Torpedo Squadron 2 (MTB RON 2), the boats were used for service testing in the Caribbean during the 1940–41 winter, after which they were transferred to the Royal Navy under the Lend-Lease Act.

In British service they were renumbered MTB 259 through 268, serving in the Mediterranean as the 10th Motor Torpedo Boat Flotilla. At least four of the boats survived the war and were returned to US custody for disposal.

Elco Specifications	
Length	70 feet
Beam	19 feet 11 inches
Displacement	33 tons
Power plant	Three 1,200 hp Packard liquid-cooled engines
Armament	Two twin .50-caliber Dewandre machine gun turrets, and four Mk. VII torpedoes
Speed	39 knots
Range	550 miles
Crew	17

PT-10 was the first series-produced, standardized PT boat built for the Navy. Manufactured by Elco and based on the Scott-Paine design, the keel for PT-10 was laid down on February 26, 1940. PT-10 and its sister boats measured 70 feet overall.

PT-10, suspended from the launching crane, is about to be launched on August 20, 1940. The boat would not be fully completed until November 4, 1940, by which time the armament, aft cabin, and other components not shown here were installed.

PT-10, shown here off Manhattan, New York, was placed in service on November 7 of the same year. It was transferred to the Royal Navy on April 11, 1941, which commissioned the vessel as HMS MTB-259.

The cabin assembly for a 70-foot PT boat is nearing completion at the Elco yard. The forward cabin framework is visible, while the rear cabin has been sheathed with plywood.

The complete cabin, as installed on the 70-foot PT-10, showed a sleek form. Aft of the cabin was a pair of Dewandre power turrets. Although the Plexiglas dome provided protection for the machine guns and the gunner, the cover was susceptible to fogging, which impaired the gunners' vision. For this reason, the covers were eventually deleted.

Visible in this view of the forward port corner of the engine room of an early Elco PT boat is one of the boat's three Packard V-12 marine engines. The Packard logo is clearly visible on the valve cover. At right are the engine controls, as well as a ladder and a fire extinguisher.

After the initial trials of 1941, Packard Marine engines such as this one were the power plant of choice for all US PT boats, most often the 4M-2500 model. The 2500-series Packard V-12 supercharged marine engines such as this one developed between 1,200 and 1,500 horsepower at 2,400 rpm, depending on the submodel.

Several Elco 70-foot PT boats of Motor Torpedo Boat Squadron 2 are visiting the Washington Navy Yard around December 1940 or January 1941. The boat with the low-profile charthouse and the smaller turret enclosures on the left side of the second pair of boats is PT-9. In the background are the presidential yacht USS *Potomac* (AG-25: *left*) and USS *Cuyahoga* (AG-26), the tender and escort for USS *Potomac*. *Naval History and Heritage Command*

The 70-foot PT-10 to PT-19 boats proved a learning experience both for Elco and the Navy. With them, the Navy found the 70-foot boats unable to accommodate four 21-inch torpedo tubes. PT-12, shown here making speed with its turrets covered, along with the rest of the PT-10 to PT-19 series, were transferred to the Royal Navy. PT-12 served with the 10th MTB Flotilla as HMS MTB 261 until decommissioned in December 1944 at Alexandria, Egypt.

CHAPTER 2
Elco 77-Foot Boats

In July 1940, the Navy Bureau of Ordnance recommended that future PT boats be armed with 21-inch torpedo tubes, rather then the 18-inch tubes found on the 70-foot Elco boats. The larger torpedo tubes were also longer, which required a longer boat.

Construction of the larger boats was approved by the General Board, with the suggestion that twenty-four of these boats be built with funds budgeted through the $50,000,000 for small craft approved for the fiscal year beginning July 1, 1940. A contract to this effect was signed with Elco on September 17, 1940. Subsequently, a further twenty-four were ordered, as well as the contract for the 70-foot boats being modified such that PT-20 was built to the new design as well.

Since the boats previously assigned to Motor Torpedo Boat Squadrons 1 and 2 all had been transferred to the British, the Chief of Naval Operations ordered that the two squadrons be reequipped with the 77-foot boats as they were delivered by Elco.

Squadron 1 was to be assigned PTs 21, 23, 25, 27, 29, and 31, while Squadron 2 received PTs 20, 22, 24, 26, 28, 30, and 32.

These squadrons immediately made a number of suggestions concerning modifications to their boats and changes in future production. At the top of the list was the request for self-sealing gas tanks. Other desired changes were an increase in visibility from the pilothouse, simplified deckhouse construction, improvement of the midships section to eliminate waste space, and a number of ordnance improvements, particularly concerning the mechanical turrets, which exhibited a number of problems.

The 77-foot boats became the first PT boats to see combat under an American flag on December 7, 1941. Boats PT-20 through 25, assigned to RON 1, were tied up at the US submarine base at Pearl Harbor. On that fateful Sunday morning, two of PT-23's gunners claimed two Japanese aircraft downed.

Elco Specifications	
Length	77 feet
Beam	19 feet 11 inches
Displacement	33 tons
Power plant	Three 1,200 hp Packard liquid-cooled engines
Armament	Two twin .50-caliber Elco machine gun turrets and four Mk. VII torpedoes. Provision for two Lewis machine guns mounted on either side of the pilothouse.
Speed	39 knots
Range	550 miles
Crew	17

In order to address several of the shortcomings of the earlier 70-foot PT boats, the Elco 77-foot PT boat was introduced in 1940. The Navy issued a contract for two dozen of the larger boats, to be numbered 21 through 44. At the same time, the earlier contract was modified so that PT-20 would be completed to the new specifications as well. *Naval History and Heritage Command*

PT-20, the first of the 77-foot boats, speeds across the water. Along with having hulls 7 feet longer than the preceding PT-10 class, these boats had longer trunk cabins and charthouses. The longer hull accommodated four torpedo tubes, which in this case are protected by waterproof covers.

PT-28, an Elco 77-foot motor torpedo boat, was laid down at Bayonne, New Jersey, on February 20, 1941, was launched on May 20 of that year, and was completed on June 30, 1941. It served successively in Motor Torpedo Boat Squadrons 2 and 1 and was serving with the latter when it was present during the Japanese attack on Pearl Harbor on December 7, 1941. The boat was destroyed in a storm in Dora Harbor, Alaska, on January 12, 1943. As seen in this photo, PT-28 had two torpedo tubes, a machine gun on a pedestal mount by the forward starboard corner of the charthouse, and enclosed turrets.

Several 77-foot PT boats are being assembled in this view of the Elco Naval Division plant in Bayonne, New Jersey. The two hulls in the foreground of this 1941 scene are upside down, and the diagonal planking is being fastened to the wooden framing.

A team of workmen are installing a section of deck on this 77-foot boat. The deck on these boats was made of mahogany plywood, whereas the 70-foot boats had used two layers of 3/16-inch mahogany planks.

At least thirteen PT boats are visible in this photograph documenting their construction at the Elco factory. These appear to be 77-foot boats with the four-panel windshield configuration at the fronts of the chart houses. The signs on the railings on the platform in the foreground are cautionary ones.

With the introduction of the 77-foot boats, the Dewandre turrets found on the 70-foot boats were replaced by hydraulically powered, Plexiglas-covered turrets of Elco's own design. While the 77-foot boats were designed for four Mk. 18-1 torpedo tubes to be mounted two per side, due to shortages of the tubes the first boats of the 77-foot boats were completed without them. The tubes, when installed, could fire Mk. 8-3C and Mk. 8-3D 21-inch torpedoes. Alternatively, type C depth charge racks could be mounted. Because of the successful trial of the 77-foot boat in the "Plywood Derby," an additional twenty-four boats were ordered.

The newly designed machine gun installation of the 77-foot boats is shown to good advantage in this photo taken during training. In the background can be seen depth charges on their racks.

Unlike the massive galleys found aboard battleships and aircraft carriers, the galley aboard a PT boat was compact to the point of being cramped. Nevertheless, the cook could turn out adequate meals for the vessel's crew.

PT boats messed together. The close quarters, as well as the stifling heat of the Pacific, meant that the crews, while disciplined, were much less formal than was often the case aboard larger warships.

One of the most famous PT boaters was Lt. (later Vice Admiral) John D. Bulkeley, seen here aboard PT-64 in 1942. As commander of Motor Torpedo Boat Squadron 3, Bulkeley evacuated Gen. Douglas MacArthur and his family and staff from the Philippines aboard 77-foot PT boats. *National Archives*

PT-41, the Elco 77-foot boat that Lt. John D. Bulkeley Jr., commanding officer of Squadron 3, used to evacuate MacArthur, was photographed stowed on a tanker en route to the Philippines in the summer of 1941, before its brush with fame.

PT-39 rolls through the streets of New York during a war bonds parade and rally. This boat had served with Squadrons 2 and 3(2) in the Pacific, and its torpedo tubes had been replaced with Mk. 13 torpedoes in drop racks.

PT-59, an Elco 77-foot motor torpedo boat, has become grounded on a reef off the western coast of Guadalcanal on February 11, 1943, while engaged in a mission for Army intelligence to investigate the sunken Japanese submarine I-1. Some of the wreckage of the sub is to the left. Gen. Alexander M. Patch is aboard the boat, standing to the front of the charthouse. *National Archives*

After the sinking of PT-109 in September 1943 Lt. (j.g.) John F. Kennedy was given command of PT-59. Based at Tulagi in the Solomon Islands, PT-59 served with Squadrons 4 and 2. Later, it was converted to a gunboat and ultimately reclassified as a small boat and was used for dehydration and preservation tests at the Philadelphia Navy Yard, where this photo was taken in March 1945.

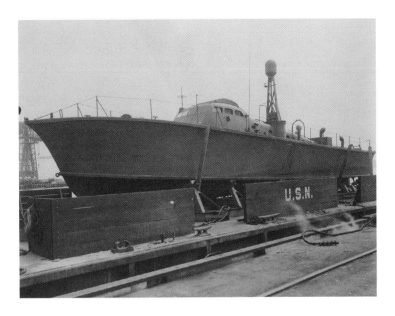

By the time ex-PT-59 was being used for experiments in Philadelphia, it was equipped with a collapsible antenna.

The 77-foot boats, like virtually all PT boats, were powered by a trio of Packard Marine engines. The engines were staggered in the engine room so as to reduce the beam of the vessel.

While some of the equipment had been removed from the charthouse prior to this photo being taken in March 1945 during the preservation tests, the basic interior structure remains visible.

The large tubing is used to supply seawater to the exhaust manifold cooling jacket.

In this forward view of the starboard side of the crew's quarters, racks are visible suspended from the overhead.

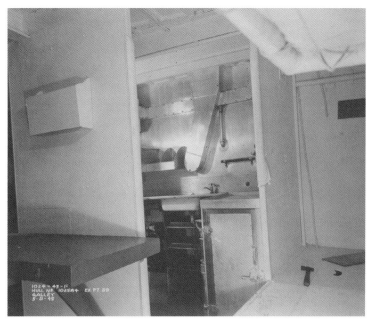

The diminutive galley featured a sink and refrigerator.

Former PT-47 was also used for dehydration and preservation tests, and this view from March 1945 shows off the propellers, struts, shafts, and rudders of a 77-foot Elco boat.

Seen here at the fueling dock at Pearl Harbor in April 1942, PT-42 had been commissioned and assigned to Motor Torpedo Boat Squadron 2 on July 22, 1941. In August of the same year, it was transferred to Squadron 1. Four depth charges are visible in the stern-mounted roll-off rack.

A nest of 80-foot Elco PT boats is secured to a dock at an unidentified harbor. Note the recognition stars on the tops of the two nearest day cabins and the subtle differences in the designs of the two radomes and their masts in the foreground. Several of the boats in the background are armed with 40 mm Bofors gun mounts.

Camouflage-painted PT-68, attached to Motor Torpedo Boat Squadron (RON) 8, is moored at the Morobe PT Boat Base in New Guinea waters in late summer 1943. This boat ran aground October 3, 1943, and after removing its crew, an accompanying PT boat destroyed PT-68 to prevent its capture.

There are various mixed arrangements of torpedo tubes and depth charges visible on the RON 8 boats tied up at the Morobe PT Boat Base in late 1943. In the foreground is the aft section of a late-model PT-20–68-class boat with a 20 mm gun; the deck stiffeners were added late in the production run.

In a view from the foredeck of an 80-foot Elco PT Boat, an Elco 77-foot PT boat (*near*) and an Elco 80-foot PT boat from Motor Torpedo Boat Squadron 8 take advantage of the camouflage offered by overhanging trees at the Morobe PT Boat Base, Papua New Guinea, around late 1943. On the deck in the foreground is a depth charge; a cover is installed over the mouth of the torpedo tube of this RON 8 80-foot boat. RON 8 operated 77-foot boats 66 through 68. *National Archives*

Two PT-boats, with an Elco 77-footer in the background, are negotiating a coastal channel at an unidentified location, likely in the South or Southwest Pacific. Several more PT boats are moored along the shoreline in the center background. In the right foreground is one of the lead boat's .50-caliber machine guns in full elevation. Farther aft is the depression rail for the 20 mm cannon on the fantail; the ammunition magazine mounted on that gun is visible.

CHAPTER 3
Higgins 78-Foot Boats

As mentioned in the introduction, once the Navy held its second "Plywood Derby," the first order was placed with Higgins. Higgins Industries was owned by Andrew Jackson Higgins, an immodest man confident in his firm's talent, both in engineering and production. Having been contracted to build PT-6 to the design of the famed yacht design firm of Sparkman and Stevens, Higgins observed what he felt were a number of flaws in the design. With the Navy unwilling to allow the changes he felt necessary, he chose to build a second PT-6, using his own money and, notably, his own design. The Higgins-designed boat was extremely well received during the course of competition.

With the edict for longer boats, Higgins returned to the drawing board and created PT-70, his "dream boat." It was this boat that the General Board recommended: "suitably reduced in size to carry such ordnance loads as are required by our navy be considered acceptable for immediate construction."

Higgins engineers redesigned their boat, and in October 1941 the firm received an initial contract for twenty-four vessels. The Higgins design, although lacking the graceful lines of the Elco, was notably rugged. Further, the Higgins boats were recognized as being more maneuverable, although the ride was a bit wetter when compared to the 80-foot Elco boats. For the motor machinists mates, the Higgins engine room was larger than that of the Elco as well, which allowed all three Packard 4M-2500 1,200-horsepower V-12 engines to be set up for direct drive.

Although only 209 of the 78-foot Higgins PTs were built, in contrast to Elco's output of 326 of its 80-foot boats, today far more survive. During the war, fifty-six of the Higgins boats were exported to the USSR and twenty-two were sent to the United Kingdom under Lend-Lease. The remainder served with the US Navy, comprising twelve squadrons.

As the war wore on, the weight and armament of the Higgins boats increased steadily, with late-production boats including a pair of eight-tube rocket launchers as well as 40 mm, 20 mm, and .50-caliber guns.

Higgins Specifications	
Length	78 feet
Beam	19 feet 11 inches
Displacement	43 tons
Power plant	Three 1,200 hp Packard liquid-cooled engines
Armament	Originally, four 21-inch torpedoes, one 40 mm mount, and two twin .50-caliber machine guns; PT-209 shown here, rearmed: one 40 mm mount, four 21-inch torpedoes, two twin .50-caliber machine guns, one 37 mm mount, and one 20 mm mount
Speed	39 knots
Range	550 miles
Crew	17

Higgins submitted the PT-70, a 70-foot boat, as its entry in the "Plywood Derby," the US Navy's 1941 competition to select designs for PT boats. In the first Plywood Derby, PT-70 performed adequately in preliminary speed tests but had to drop out of the 190-mile high-speed race because of structural damage to the frame and deck. After being repaired, PT-70 took part in the second derby, coming in second in the speed test but again sustaining damage to the deck and hull planks.

Higgins PT-70 is seen from above, likely during manufacturer's trials, carrying naval and civilian personnel. While lacking operational weapons, the PT-70 design included a charthouse, open bridge, two machine gun turrets toward the front of the boat, and a fairly uncluttered mid- and afterdeck. The configuration of turrets aft of the bridge is similar to that employed on the early-production Higgins PT boats, but the turret on the afterdeck was not a feature that went into production. Mockups of two depth charge racks are on the fantail.

Following an early October 1941 conference between the Navy and potential PT builders Elco, Higgins, and Huckins, Higgins Industries was awarded a contract to build twenty-four boats, numbered PT-71 through PT-94. Here, the lead vessel of the class, PT-71, is shown as built, with the enlarged bridge and the turrets mounted at the rear of an extended superstructure to the rear of the bridge. This boat was completed in July 1942; by September 1943, PT-71 had been remodeled, with the superstructure truncated and the turrets moved to abreast of the bridge.

Higgins 78-foot PT-72 was constructed with the elongated superstructure aft of the charthouse, with the turrets positioned at the rear of the superstructure. The port turret is visible in this photograph, slightly aft of the front of the forward torpedo tube. This is one of the Higgins PT boats that served in the Aleutians with MTB Squadron 16, and in 1944 the boat was transferred to MTB RON 2(2) for service with the OSS in the English Channel.

PT-86, a 78-foot motor torpedo boat, is under construction outdoors at Higgins Industries Inc., New Orleans, Louisiana, on October 29, 1942. The placard leaning against the turret reads "P-T 86." Two anchors are lying on the deck to the front of the charthouse.

78 FT. PT 71-94, 197-254
PORT QUARTER VIEW PT-75,76
CONTRACT NOs 94729 AND 94729 OPTION 1
HIGGINS INDUSTRIES, INC.
NEW ORLEANS, LA., U.S.A.
8-3-42

Construction of 78-foot PT boats at Higgins also was carried out indoors, as was the case with PT-75 and PT-76 in this photograph taken on August 3, 1942. As constructed, several of the Higgins PT boats numbered in the 70s and 80s had superstructure sides that extended well to the rear of the bridge, a rear bulkhead for the bridge (with a hatch on the starboard side), and turrets mounted at the rear of the superstructure. On the deck of the boat to the left, unpainted foundations for the torpedo tubes have been installed; they are made of laminated wood. On the boat to the right, the weldments for supports for the torpedo tubes have been mounted on the foundations.

Another August 3, 1942, photograph taken at Higgins Industries shows 78-foot PT boats under assembly. The foredecks of two boats are in the foreground. The three boats in the next row are (*left to right*) PT-77, PT-80, and PT-82. Placards leaning against the smoke generators on the afterdecks give the manufacturer's number, the date the keel was laid down, and the PT boat number. All three boats have the extended superstructures with the turrets to their rears.

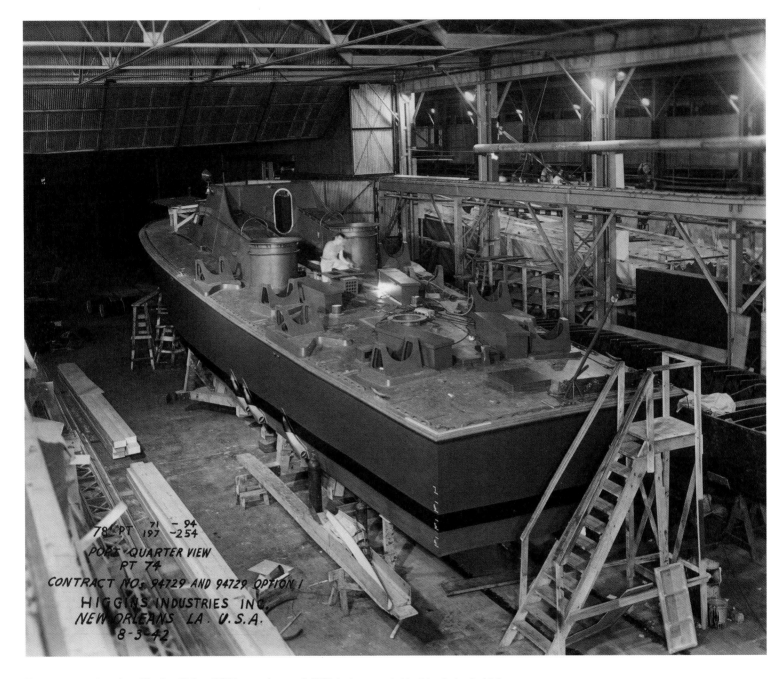

The progress of work on Higgins 78-foot PT-74 up to August 3, 1942, is documented in this photo. A ship's bell and a searchlight are mounted on the left side of the bridge. The hatch through the rear bulkhead of the bridge is easily detected, since there is a light-colored border around it.

A member of MTB Squadron 16 walks past two Higgins PT boats moored to a dock at New Orleans around early 1943. The boat to the left is PT-221, with canvas covers over the turret and the machine guns. Note the draft marks on the bow of the closer boat

The bridge (sometimes called the cockpit) of PT-221 is seen from above the engine room hatch (*bottom center*) around early 1943. On the deck to the right of the crewman in the hatch to the charthouse is an open hatch to the wardroom. Two cowl ventilators are on each side of the engine room hatch.

Two Higgins PT boats of MTB RON 16 at a dock in New Orleans are viewed from aft around early 1943. Canvas covers are over the 20 mm guns on the fantails and the twin .50-caliber machine gun turrets, and a good view is available of the curved air-impulse chamber on the top of each of the 21-inch, Mk. 19 Mod 4 torpedo tubes.

Chief Motor Machinist Mate Alfred G. Abeckerle, of MTB Squadron 16, stood on the fantail of a Higgins PT boat to take this color photo during the squadron's movement from New Orleans to the Motor Torpedo Boat Squadrons Training School, at Melville, Rhode Island. In the background is another Higgins PT boat.

A crewman on a Higgins PT boat from MTB RON 16 is manning the starboard turret. Linked rounds of .50-caliber ammunition are dangling from the feed chute on the side of the left gun. Below the guns is a spent-casing chute in the form of a large-diameter flex hose.

One of the first places that the US Navy deployed the Higgins boats was in the Aleutians, where these three examples were seen on June 21, 1943. Tied alongside USS *Gillis* (AVD-12), a seaplane tender-destroyer, are three boats of Squadron 13, while at the stern is a PBY Catalina. Each of the boats has been equipped with some form of a windshield. *National Archives*

MTB Squadron 13 consisted of PTs 73 through 84, all Higgins 78-foot models. In this companion to the previous photo can be seen three more of the RON 13 boats tied up on the other side of the USS *Gillis* at Massacre Bay, Attu, Aleutian Islands. *Naval History and Heritage Command*

Four Higgins 78-foot PT boats are moored together, including one at the far end with an early-model radar mast and a group of sailors on the foredeck. The Higgins boats were stockier than the Elcos and had much more clear deck space, having only a charthouse and no day cabin. The .50-caliber machine gun turrets were mounted opposite each other to the rear of the bridge, rather than staggered as on the Elco boats. *National Archives*

At a submarine base on Kodiak Island in the Aleutians, several PT boats of MTB RON 16 are tied to a dock. The closest boat suffered considerable damage to the charthouse when a huge wave struck it during a storm; it was to be repaired at an extensive carpentry shop at Kodiak.

While assigned to duty in the Aleutian Islands, this Higgins PT boat commanded by Lt. Boon of MTB Squadron 16 collided with a destroyer, causing damage to its bow, which in this photo has been patched with plywood. The crewman in the parka leaning over the hatch on the bow is Warrant Officer Henry Cales. On the port turret is a cowboy hat insignia.

On the port side of the open hatch leading down to the crew quarters on a Higgins PT boat assigned to MTB RON 16 is lashed a life raft. PT boat crewmen sometimes got rid of these rafts as an inconvenient encumbrance and obstacle. In the raft is a large can of survival rations and equipment. Next to the raft is a boat hook.

Tommy Allison, of MTB RON 16, is in the port turret of a Higgins PT boat of Motor Torpedo Boat Squadron 16, alongside a dock at a base in the Aleutians. The curved grips of the gun mount enabled the gunner to quickly manipulate the elevation of the .50-caliber machine guns.

A Higgins PT boat of MTB Squadron 16 is leaving a base in the Aleutians at the start of a patrol mission. This squadron was stationed in the Aleutians from August 1943 to May 1944.

When Squadron 16 deployed in column, taking up the rear of the column was PT-224. Thus, the name "Tail End" was a natural. The pinup "nose art" was painted by Paul Stevens. The vertical pipe at right held water in which to submerge the barrel of the bow 20 mm gun in the event it began to overheat, which would cause jamming.

Two torpedo tubes and two depth charge racks are mounted on each side of this Higgins PT, shown in Alaskan waters. A ready ammunition box for the aft 20 mm cannon is mounted between the two depth charges. The characteristic submerged, side-mounted Higgins exhaust is churning up the water alongside the boat.

On a dock adjacent to the Higgins PT boat of Lieutenant Boone, Torpedoman Bob Carlson prepares a Mk. 13 torpedo. The "Base 13" stenciled on the side of the dolly refers to PT Boat Base 13 at Casco Cove in Massacre Bay, Attu, in the Aleutians.

A group of torpedoman's mates service a Mk. 13 torpedo in Alaska. The compartment holding the gyro and starting gears and depth-setting mechanism is open, and the second man from the right is adjusting the mechanism within. *National Archives*

After service in the Aleutians, Squadron 13 went to Puget Sound Navy Yard, Bremerton, Washington, where the boats were overhauled and updated prior to being sent to the Southwest Pacific. When built, this boat's .50-caliber machine gun turrets were at the rear of an elongated superstructure. Later, the superstructure aft of the charthouse was remodeled, and the turrets were moved to the typical locations abreast of the bridge. It was in Puget Sound that these photos of PT-77 were taken on July 3, 1944, showing the results of the overhaul. *National Archives*

The modifications included the replacement of the torpedo tubes with lighter drop racks, a reduction in the number of torpedoes carried, the installation of a 40 mm Bofors gun on the fantail, a 20 mm gun to the foredeck, and two tripod machine gun mounts amidships. The addition of radar required a mast for the apparatus as well. *National Archives*

The amidships gun mounts remained in the as-built positions. Here, the guns are locked at maximum elevation, with the weather covers in place. On the fantail, an A-frame bipod serves as a travel lock for the 40 mm gun barrel. On the port side of the stern is the bottle-shaped smoke discharger, still in its factory-installed position. *National Archives*

An extension on the 40 mm gun cover protects the gun's auto loader. Even at idle, the exhaust from the big Packards caused significant bubbling of the water alongside the boat. *National Archives*

The charthouse windows were painted over in order to prevent glare, which could give away the boat's position. Dispatched to the Philippines with the rest of RON 13, along with PT-79, PT-77 was lost on February 1, 1945, when USS *Conyngham* (DD-371) and USS *Lough* (DE-586) mistook the PTs for enemy kamikaze boats and opened fire off Talin Point, Batangas Province, Luzon. While both PTs were sunk, fortunately there were no casualties. *National Archives*

Production of the second group of Higgins 78-foot PT boats, the PT-197-254 class, ran from June 23, 1942, when the first hull was laid down, until June 16, 1943, when the final boat of the class, PT-254, was finished. When built, these boats differed little from their predecessors, the PT-71 through 94 class; however, both classes were subjected to many later modifications and upgrades, such as the addition of radar and 40 mm Bofors guns. *National Archives*

Shown here just after delivery, PT-200 is equipped with two sets of twin .50-caliber machine guns, four torpedo tubes, and a 20 mm Oerlikon cannon on the fantail. During service, Navy yards would retrofit many boats in the PT-197–254 class with drop racks rather than tubes for Mk. 13 torpedoes, as well as radar masts, 40 mm guns, and other weapons. *National Archives*

PT-200 was built before radar equipment became standard; thus its mast, mounted aft of the bridge, was stubby and had a navigation light at the top. Higgins mounted their torpedo tubes set at 12 degrees from the centerline, which permitted them to be launched clear of the boat, without requiring the turntable mechanism Elco used to achieve the same goal. PT-200 was ultimately assigned to Squadron 4, the PT boat training unit at Melville, Rhode Island. It was in this service that it was lost on February 22, 1944, after colliding with an unknown object off Newport, Rhode Island. *National Archives*

The hulls of Higgins 78-foot PT boats are under production. To the left is PT-199, while to the right is PT-197. The design of the frame for the upper deck of the Higgins 78-foot PT boats is evident. The bottom and sides of the hull and the deck were constructed of two layers of mahogany planks, with marine glue and fabric between the layers to bond them. The planks on the bows above the chine are arranged at a nearly vertical angle, roughly parallel to the angle of the stem; below the chine, the planks are approximately horizontal. *National Archives*

Lined up two abreast during assembly at Higgins Industries' City Park Plant, in New Orleans, are 78-foot PT boats. The boat to the front right is PT-267. The hull of the boat to the left above the chine appears to have been painted, while the entire hull of the boat to its right has not been painted. The boat in the right row to the rear has advanced only to the framing of the hull. To the rear of the building is a sign that reminds the workers, "The guy who relaxes is helping the Axis!" *Naval History and Heritage Command*

PT-201, the fifth boat in the class, rests on a railroad flatcar prior to completion. Only the charthouse and two storage boxes have been mounted on the otherwise clean deck. Visible just below the waterline are the portside engine exhausts. *National Archives*

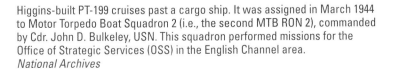

Higgins-built PT-199 cruises past a cargo ship. It was assigned in March 1944 to Motor Torpedo Boat Squadron 2 (i.e., the second MTB RON 2), commanded by Cdr. John D. Bulkeley, USN. This squadron performed missions for the Office of Strategic Services (OSS) in the English Channel area. *National Archives*

Personnel of PT-199 are gathered on the bridge and the starboard turret off the Normandy coast, visible in the background, on D-Day. The flag with four stars flying from the starboard side of the mast indicates that a full admiral is aboard. *National Archives*

During a mass commissioning ceremony for newly completed 78-foot PT boats at Higgins Industries' Canal Plant, New Orleans, on June 28, 1942, the three boats in the foreground are, *left to right*, PT-281, PT-277, and PT-288. A standardized camouflage pattern has been painted on these boats. On PT-277, a Navy officer and several Catholic clergymen are seen departing from the foredeck and are about to move over to PT-281. *Naval History and Heritage Command*

Two US Navy 78-foot Higgins PT boats are moored to a dock at the advanced PT boat base at Maddalena, Sardinia, around late 1943. A captured Italian corvette is on the other side of the dock. The bombed-out building to the left subsequently was repaired and used as a PT boat engineering repair facility. *Naval History and Heritage Command*

PT-211 of Squadron 15, seen here at the PT boat base at Bastia, Corsica, in February 1944, was commanded by Lt. (j.g.) Page H. Tulloch. PT-211 featured several modifications, ranging from the installation of radar with an early-model radar mast, to the installation of four sets of forward-firing rocket launchers, each holding four rockets. It was hoped that these weapons would be useful against German F-lighters, flak boats active in the Mediterranean, but were used only twice. *National Archives*

This Mediterranean-based Higgins 78-foot PT boat has been painted in a zebra-stripe camouflage scheme. These stripes are much wider than those found on Elco PT boats. On top of the chart is a radio direction-finding antenna. *National Archives*

After the overhaul and refit of Motor Torpedo Boat Squadron 16's boats at Bremerton, the unit was sent to the Southwest Pacific. Here, PT-221 is being unloaded from the LST that transported the boat into the waters off Manus Island in the Admiralty Islands, New Guinea. From Manus, in September 1944 the squadron shifted to Mios Woende in the Netherlands East Indies (modern Indonesia). From this angle the new camouflage scheme of the boat can be seen, as well as the 20 mm cannon and two ammunition boxes mounted on the foredeck, an early-model radar mast (shown lowered) that has been installed aft of the bridge, as well as the 40 mm Bofors gun that replaced the 20 mm cannon on the fantail.

At an advanced US Navy base at Mios Woendi, an island southeast of Indonesia, natives in an outrigger canoe talk with members of the crew of a Higgins PT boat of MTB Squadron 16. On the port side of the deck is a smoke generator. Draft numbers are painted in white on the stern.

In an undated photograph, officers of MTB Squadron 16 confer at the PT boat base at Mangarin Bay, Mindoro, the Philippines. The boats in the foreground have 40 mm Bofors mounts on the afterdecks. The origin and purpose of the white objects on the nearby boats are not clear; they are shaped like day cabins but do not match known examples

Part of the PT-265–313 class of 78-foot Higgins boats, the first hull of which was laid November 23, 1942, PT-286 displays a placard proclaiming that its construction was sponsored by the war bonds and stamps purchases of the citizens of Montgomery County, Illinois. *National Archives*

This overhead view of PT-285, assigned to Squadron 23, was taken during its shakedown cruise off the entrance to the Miami Yacht Harbor, Florida, showing details of general arrangement of the PT-265-313 class. The final boat of this class was completed January 31, 1944.

Commissioned on January 26, 1944, PT-309, "Oh Frankie," was assigned to Motor Torpedo Boat Squadron 22 in the Mediterranean. While there, it supported of the Allied invasion of the Italian island of Elba on June 16–17, 1944. In this view, it is equipped with an early-model radar mast and a 20 mm cannon on the foredeck. After the German surrender, the squadron, including PT-309, was shipped by stateside for reconditioning prior to redeployment in the Pacific. Japan surrendered before the unit shipped back out, and PT-309 was declared surplus and transferred to the War Shipping Administration on June 18, 1948. In 1960 it was sold, and it still survives today, displayed at the National Museum of the Pacific War, Fredericksburg, Texas.

PT-461, a Higgins 78-foot boat, was laid down on September 13, 1943, at Higgins' New Orleans works and was launched on October 30 of that year. After completion of her fitting out on March 28, 1944, she was assigned to Motor Torpedo Boat Squadron 30. PT-461 served in the English Channel from June 1944 to June 1945. Note the boat stored upside-down on the deck, and the camouflage paint scheme.

A camouflaged 78-foot Higgins, probably PT-453 of Squadron 30, kicks up spray as it speeds along. With no Bofors guns or torpedoes mounted, the deck of this midproduction Higgins PT boat is open and uncluttered compared with the Elco 80-foot PT boats, which were crammed with a day cabin, after turret, and engine room hatch/ventilator. The machine gun turrets of this late Higgins have been shifted a bit aft of their former locations next to the bridge. Aft of the bridge is an early-style collapsible radar mast with radome. *National Archives*

Rising above PT-453's deck amidships are four adjustable vents that supply air to the engine room. Along the edge of the deck are a pair of roll-off torpedo racks, and at the stern is a smoke generator.
National Archives

Production of the PT-625–660 class of Higgins 78-foot boats began on May 17, 1944, and continued to August 27, 1945. Here, PT-625 is suspended from a hoist as it is being lowered into the waters adjacent to the Higgins plant. Stenciled on the bow are draft marks.

PT-631 was photographed in New Orleans before being shipped to Puget Sound and subsequently transferred to Russia. But for four boats, this entire class of boats was supplied to the Soviet Union. Notably, charthouse windows, which had been painted over for some time, were at last eliminated. The boat is fitted with a late-model radar mast.

The PT-625–660-class boats left the Higgins factory with a Mk. 50 5-inch rocket launcher mounted on each side of the main deck forward of the charthouse. Elevation of the launcher was manual by means of a crank near the top, but the eight rockets in each were fired electrically from the bridge. While the launcher swung out from the boat for firing, the direction of the boat controlled traverse.

The port Mk. 50 5-inch rocket launcher of PT-631 is seen in its stowed position, with the muzzles of the tubes facing aft. The crank at the top of the launcher mount controls elevation, and the heavy cable rising from the deck connects the ignition circuit to the bridge. In the background, near the bow, the 37 mm autocannon with its magazine, mount, and foundation is visible.

Additional armament of the PT-631 included roll-off torpedo racks, a 20 mm Oerlikon cannon mounted amidships, and a 40 mm Bofors gun on the fantail. Below the depression rail, which protected the 40 mm crew, is a large 40 mm ammunition stowage locker. The two aft deck vents characteristic of early Higgins PT boats are no longer installed.

Built by Higgins Industries, of New Orleans, PT-658 was delivered and accepted on July 31, 1945, and is a good example of a very late Higgins PT boat. After the war it served as a patrol boat for several missile ranges along the Pacific coast. The boat was in private hands from 1958 until being donated to Save the PT Boat Inc., of Portland, Oregon, which restored the boat to its original standards. Now, PT-658 is one of two surviving, operational PT boats and may be visited at the PT-658 Heritage Museum in Portland.
Jim Alexander

Armaments on the foredeck of PT-658 are a 37 mm Oldsmobile automatic cannon (*center*) and a 20 mm cannon, both of which are on tripod stands. To the sides are Mk. 50 eight-tube rocket launchers. The planks of the hull are visible in this lighting and at this angle. *Jim Alexander*

On the afterdeck of PT-658 is a 40 mm antiaircraft gun mount. Forward of that gun is a 20 mm antiaircraft cannon, pointing upward. Four torpedoes are in their racks on the sides of the deck. On the rear of the deck are two depth charges and a smoke generator. *Jim Alexander*

PT-658 chugs along a river, with passengers onboard. The camouflage is a replica of the Measure 31-20L scheme the boat reportedly was finished in when delivered in 1945. *Jim Alexander*

The starboard Mk. 50 rocket launcher on PT-658 is viewed. Each launcher had eight tubes for 5-inch, spin-stabilized rockets, giving the PT-boat a firepower capability similar to that of a US Navy destroyer's 5-inch guns. This rocket mount appears to be a replica or an incomplete original.

The engine room of a surviving Higgins 78-foot PT boat is viewed looking forward. In the right foreground is the front end of the center of three Packard 4M-2500 engines. To the front of this engine are the port and the starboard 4M-2500 engines. On the forward bulkhead of the engine room is the instrument panel; the yellow plumbing fixtures below the instrument panel are part of the fuel system.

Higgins-built PT-305 served in the Mediterranean from 1944 to the end of the war. Following World War II, the boat worked as a charter boat, oyster boat, and tour boat in New York, and it underwent several drastic remodelings. Since 2007, PT-305 has been a part of the National World War II Museum in New Orleans. During the war, and now, this boat was nicknamed "USS *Sudden Jerk*." *David Jackson*

During coastal and riverine operations against the Japanese, PT boat crews sometimes mounted mortars on the foredecks. PT-305 has such a setup, in the form of a 60 mm mortar, with raised foundations for the base plate and the bipod. Farther aft, on the port side of the foredeck, is a 20 mm cannon with magazine installed; the barrel is resting on an A-frame travel lock. *David Jackson*

As seen from the foredeck, a life raft is lashed to the starboard front of the charthouse. Below the raft are a locker, ventilators, and a boat hook. Above the machine gun turrets are the depression rails, which kept the gunners from accidentally firing into vital parts of the boat. *David Jackson*

The 20 mm cannon and magazine on the foredeck are seen close-up. On the front of the port side of the charthouse is a storage locker. A grab rail, painted black, runs across the upper front of the charthouse. *David Jackson*

In the corner between the port side of the charthouse and the gun turret is a red navigation light. A ventilator is attached to the rear side window of the charthouse. To each side of the radome is a so-called ski-pole antenna. *David Jackson*

The port twin .50-caliber machine gun mount is shown in detail. Affixed to the muzzles are flash suppressors. The curved grips, for maneuvering the guns at high elevation, are visible to the rear of the guns. *David Jackson*

The bridge of PT-305 is viewed from a closer perspective. To the front of the helm is a rudder-angle indicator. On the shelf above the helm are throttle and telegraph controls, to the starboard side of which is an instrument panel. To the starboard of the helm are an electrical control panel and a hatch into the charthouse. *David Jackson*

The turrets and the bridge of PT-305 are viewed from the port side of the afterdeck. In the left foreground is a single .50-caliber machine gun on a pedestal mount, with an ammunition box on the side. *David Jackson*

The 40 mm Bofors gun on the afterdeck of PT-305 is trained forward and is somewhat elevated. To the rear of the gun mount is a guardrail with built-in racks for the four-round clips of 40 mm ammunition. The gunner and the lateral pointer who aimed the weapon had ring-and-bead sights and hand cranks. *David Jackson*

Although Elco produced more PT boats than did Higgins, more of the Higgins boats survive, including PT-309, which is currently on indoor display at the National Museum of the Pacific War, Fredericksburg, Texas. A combat veteran, PT-309 wore the nickname "Oh Frankie" due to a chance meeting of its skipper and Frank Sinatra at a New York City nightclub. *Photo by author*

PT-309 saw service in the Mediterranean and was credited with sinking five enemy vessels. As displayed, with the lights on in the charthouse, it is apparent why blackout covers were required during wartime. To port of the boat's centerline is a Mk. 4 20 mm Oerlikon cannon. *Photo by author*

PT-309 is displayed as if tied up dockside at a PT base. From the "dock," this view of the aft port side of the boat exposes, *left to right*, a Mk. 13 torpedo, the aft torpedo launching rack, and a depth charge in a roll-off rack. In the distance, a mannequin is at the helm. *Photo by author*

PT-796, owned by the veteran's group PT Boats Inc., of Germantown, Tennessee, is displayed at Battleship Cove, Fall River, Massachusetts. The last Higgins PT built, PT Boats Inc. acquired the boat from the Navy, and in July 1970 it moved under its own power from Pensacola, Florida, to Memphis, Tennessee, to be part of a PT boat museum. It was later moved to Fall River, where it is displayed today indoors. *Photo by author*

PT-796 was completed on October 26, 1945, and was briefly assigned to MTB Squadron 1, operating in the Caribbean. Subsequently, it was assigned to the Navy Operational Development Force and Naval Ship Research Development Laboratory, Panama City, Florida. Its armament was removed and it was used for high-speed towing experiments. It later masqueraded as the Elco PT-109 during President Kennedy's inauguration parade, during which it was towed on a trailer, with many surviving PT-109 crewmen aboard. *Photo by author*

Restoration of PT-796 is ongoing. As mentioned, the Navy had stripped the boat of its armament in the 1940s, and the vessel had also suffered some damage from vandals in Memphis, but it is being painstakingly returned to its as-built configuration. *Photo by author*

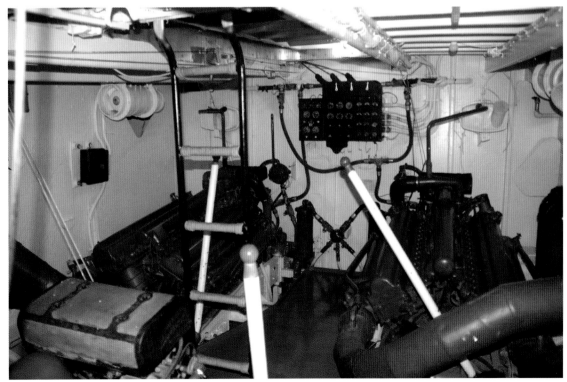

The Hellcat was an experimental 70-foot motor torpedo boat prototype built by Higgins Industries on their own initiative. It was laid down during 1942, completed on June 30, 1943, and subjected to builder's trials on Lake Pontchartrain, outside New Orleans, on June 30, 1943. The Hellcat had a sleek look, with a compact charthouse with the two turrets grouped within the confines of the rear of the cockpit. The boat was fast and maneuverable, having a maximum speed of 46 knots and the ability to reverse course in nine seconds.

After successful builder's trials of the Hellcat by Higgins Industries, the US Navy purchased the boat on August 6, 1943, designating it PT-564. The Navy assigned the boat to MTB Squadron 4 at the Motor Torpedo Boat Squadrons Training School, in Melville, Rhode Island, in November 1944. The boat is seen here after acceptance, with "USS PT-564" painted on the side of the charthouse. Despite the fact that the Hellcat delivered impressive results during the Navy trials, the boat lacked the size to lend itself to modifications as a gunboat, which was becoming a more important consideration in the latter part of World War II. Thus, the Navy did not order the Hellcat into series production.

One of the experiments conducted with the Higgins Hellcat was the mounting of four remote-controlled Browning M2 .50-caliber machine guns on the foredeck. Between these guns and their outboard sides were ammunition boxes. Photographs exist of a different configuration of ammunition boxes, with two separate, taller boxes on the deck between the two paired gun mounts. Between the two turrets, which are manned, is the folded-down radar mast. There were racks for four torpedoes, and a 20 mm antiaircraft cannon was mounted on the afterdeck.

CHAPTER 4
Huckins and Canadian Powerboats

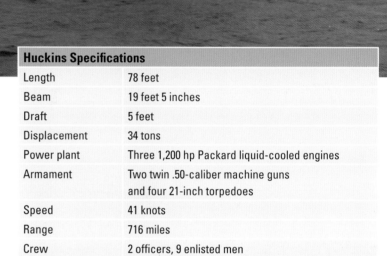

The first PT boat built by the Huckins Yacht Company of Jacksonville, Florida, was PT-69, which was the firm's entry in the "Plywood Derby" off New London, Connecticut, from July 21 to 24, 1941. The 72-foot boat was powered by a whopping four Packard 1,200-horsepower engines. *National Archives*

Huckins Yacht Company of Jacksonville, Florida, also was issued a production contract following the second Plywood Derby. The firm, led by Frank Pembroke Huckins, used its own funds and government-supplied engines to produce the 70-foot PT-69 for that competition. PT-69 proved to be one of the most maneuverable and fastest boats in the competition, but damage sustained during the trials forced it to withdraw.

That performance, however, was sufficient for the Navy to award a contract for production of eight examples of a newly designed 78-foot boat powered by three Packard 4M-2500 engines (PT-69 had used four). A second contract for ten more boats soon followed.

Three of the boats, PTs 95 through 97, were assigned to the training squadron RON 4, stationed in Melville, Rhode Island. Boats PT-98 through 102 were provided to RON 14 and were used defending the Canal Zone as well as providing advanced training. Assigned to Squadron 26, boats PT-255 through PT-264 were stationed in Hawaii, in defense of the islands.

The Canadian Powerboat Company in Montreal had been contracted to produce eight 70-foot motor torpedo boats of a Scott-Paine design for the Royal Netherlands Navy. Half of these were provided to the US Navy under reverse Lend-Lease, becoming PTs 368 through 371. The boats were assigned to Squadron 18 and saw service in the Southwest Pacific, seeing action at Dreger Harbor, Aitape, Hollandia, Wakde, and Mios Woendi, in New Guinea; at Manus in the Admiralties; and at Morotai in the Halmaheras.

Huckins Specifications

Length	78 feet
Beam	19 feet 5 inches
Draft	5 feet
Displacement	34 tons
Power plant	Three 1,200 hp Packard liquid-cooled engines
Armament	Two twin .50-caliber machine guns and four 21-inch torpedoes
Speed	41 knots
Range	716 miles
Crew	2 officers, 9 enlisted men

Canadian Powerboat Specifications

Length	70 feet
Beam	19 feet
Draft	4 feet 9 inches
Displacement	33 tons
Power plant	Three 1,500 hp Packard W-14 M2500 engines
Speed	41 knots
Armament	Two 21-inch torpedo tubes, one 37 mm mount, one 20 mm mount, and two twin .50-caliber machine guns
Range	716 miles
Crew	2 officers, 9 enlisted men

Frank Huckins's firm was the second to be awarded a contract to produce PT boats, following Higgins. PT-95 was the first boat of that contract. Unlike PT-69, the PT-95-class boats were powered by a trio of Packard engines and were 78 feet long.
National Archives

The second production Huckins boat, PT-96, was laid down on January 29, 1942, was launched in June of that year, and was placed in service on August 24, 1942. It was assigned to Motor Torpedo Squadron 4 and used for training.

PT-95 speeds away from the camera, leaving a heavy wake. Whereas Elco had expanded its Bayonne plant before the war, and with government assistance made a further expansion, and Higgins had done the same (largely in order to produce landing craft), Huckins's small plant was entirely self-funded and accordingly had a much-lower rate of production than did the others. This, along with other factors, led to the firm receiving only small contracts for PT boats. *National Archives*

PT-95 was also assigned to Motor Torpedo Squadron 4, the training squadron in Melville, Rhode Island, which with a peak of twenty-eight boats was the largest of all PT squadrons. After being struck from the Naval Register on September 13, 1945, it was stripped and scuttled off the Rhode Island coast. *National Archives*

PT-262, nicknamed "Barfly," pushes through the waters off Hawaii in the spring of 1945 while assigned to Motor Torpedo Boat Squadron 26 as part of the islands' defenses. Waterproof coverings envelop the Mk. 13 torpedoes, 20 mm cannon, and .50-caliber machine gun turrets. On the radome, the number "2" has been stenciled.

The Huckins-patent Quadraconic hull of PT-262 crosses the wake of another boat as the vessels operate in Hawaiian waters. While a waterproof cover has been installed on the 40 mm Bofors gun, the gun barrel and gunsights protrude from it.

Among those assembled on the bridge of PT-262 on Christmas Day 1944 are two officers; Lt. (j.g.) Cleveland E. Dodge and an Ens. Bruce. Resting in the waters of Pearl Harbor, the boat displays the coaming of the bridge, the slots in which are part of the wind deflector, and was similar in design to that used on Vosper motor torpedo boats.

The first group of Huckins PT boats was the class 95 through 102 boats. The second and final group was the PT-255 through PT-264 class. PT-257 was a member of this second group and served with Motor Torpedo Boat Squadron 26 on the Hawaiian Sea Frontier. It carried three successive nicknames: *Laputita*, *Miss Carriage*, and *Idiot's Delight*.

Four PT boats, numbered 368 to 371, were completed by the Canadian Power Boat Company, Montreal, Canada, in March and April 1943. The boats were built for the Dutch government but were delivered to the US Navy under reverse Lend-Lease. These 70-foot boats were based on a Scott-Paine design. All four boats were assigned to Squadron 18 in the Southwest Pacific.

Members of the crew of "Sad Sack," PT-369, gather on the bridge of their boat. Second from left is Ens. Frank Gore, skipper of the boat. Visible on the roof of the charthouse is the BN antenna of the IFF system.

CHAPTER 5
Elco 80-Foot Boats

As a result of the second Plywood Derby's evaluation, the Navy recommended several changes to the 77-foot Elco boat, as well as a revision of Elco's pricing. Elco had been notably higher than the other firms, but once the price was brought in line, the Bayonne firm was given a contract for production of a new class of 80-foot boats in late 1941.

The lead boat of this class, PT-103, was launched on May 16, 1942, and with it was launched the production of the dominant type of US PT boat of World War II. The 80-foot Elco was characterized by a nearly flat foredeck, staggered turrets, and an angular charthouse and bore little resemblance to the earlier 70-foot and 77-foot boats from the same firm. The boat, however, was powered by the same arrangement of three Packard V-12s as the previous models and, at least initially, used the same style of torpedo tubes.

The longer boats were also heavier, weighing five tons more than the 77-foot predecessors, which brought about a slightly lower top speed as well as reducing maneuverability. This was offset in part by better seakeeping characteristics.

In addition to the four torpedo tubes, armament of the early 80-foot Elco boats consisted of depth charges, .50-caliber machine guns, and a single, aft-mounted 20 mm Oerlikon cannon. Beginning with PT-115, smoke generators were added on the fantail.

Other changes made during production of successive contracts for additional 80-foot Elco boats included removing the spray shields around the engine room hatch in 1943, and redesigning the hatch to function as an air intake. Also during 1943, radar became standard equipment, and additional and more-powerful weapons began to be installed by Elco, culminating in a pair of 5-inch, eight-tube rocket launchers. This was part of a gradual shift of the vessels from torpedo boats to gunboats, and their increasing use as barge busters.

Helping to maintain speed despite the ever-increasing weight of the boats, improvements in the Packard engines brought about an increase in horsepower, first from 1,200 to 1,350 and later to 1,500.

Elco Specifications	
Length	80 feet
Beam	20 feet 8 inches
Displacement	51 tons, later 61 tons
Power plant	Three 1,200 hp Packard liquid-cooled engines
Armament (initial)	Two twin .50-caliber machine gun turrets, four torpedoes, and a 20 mm Oerlikon cannon. (late) Two twin .50-caliber machine gun turrets, four torpedoes, a 20 mm Oerlikon cannon, a 40 mm Bofors, a 37 mm Oldsmobile, and two Mk. 50 eight-tube rocket launchers
Speed	40–43 knots
Range	550 miles
Crew	17
Crew	2 officers, 9 enlisted men

The first of the 80-foot Elco PT boats, PT-103 is being lowered by launching crane into the water of Newark Bay in front of the Elco Naval Division, Electric Boat Company, Bayonne, New Jersey, on May 16, 1942.

In this view taken at the factory on August 4, 1942, PT-117 shows off the nearly flat foredeck characteristic of the PT-103 to PT-196 class. This boat is equipped with the early-type mast.

The staggered twin .50-caliber machine gun installations used on Elco 80-foot boats are visible on PT-117. The forward turret is on the starboard side of the charthouse, and the aft turret is on the port side of the day cabin.

Rising through the waterline of PT-117 are the six mufflers for the Packard Marine engines. PT-117 ultimately served with Motor Torpedo Boat Squadron 6 under the nickname "Munda Morn." It was attacked and destroyed by Japanese aircraft on August 1, 1943, at Rendova in the Solomon Islands.

The aft torpedo tubes of PT-107 have been replaced by eight depth charges and ammunition-ready boxes. With those weapons, as well as two tubes for Mk. 8 torpedoes, the boat is equipped for antisubmarine operations during a tour of duty in the Panama Canal Zone. The foredeck remains clean and uncluttered.

FOREMAST
FORD KINGPOST
CONFIDENTIAL
S. S. JOSEPH STANTON - PT BOAT STOWAGE
SHELTER DK - STB'D SIDE - FOR'D
NORFOLK NAVY YARD, PORTSMOUTH, VA.
SERIAL Nº 3538 (42) - 8-20-42

This is PT-109, later lost along with two of its crew while under the command of Lt. (j.g.) John F. Kennedy when the PT collided with the Japanese destroyer *Amagiri* on August 5, 1943. The publicity surrounding this is considered by many to have been instrumental in Kennedy's successful White House bid later.

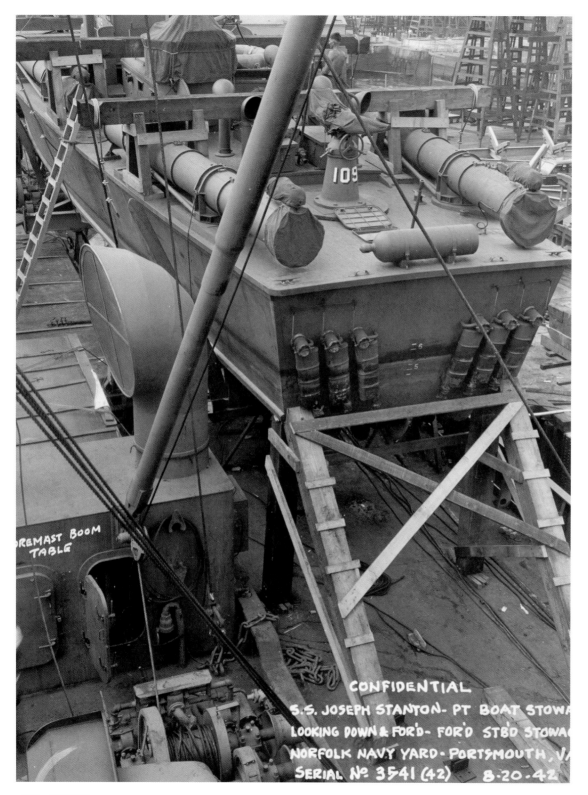

In another view of PT-109 loaded aboard the USS *Joseph Stanton* for transport, the smoke generator, aft 20 mm mount, and mufflers are clearly visible.

A crewman mans the port turret of Elco-built PT-140 during a training exercise out of the Motor Torpedo Boat Squadrons Training School, Melville, Rhode Island, in the late summer of 1943. *National Archives*

Two Elco PT boats are making a high-speed run off a mountainous coastline during World War II. To the left of the turret in the foreground is the cradle for the radome when the mast was lowered. Faintly visible on the afterdeck of the boat from which this photo was taken is a 40 mm Bofors cannon mount. *National Archives*

A three-man crew is serving a 20 mm antiaircraft cannon on the afterdeck of an Elco 80-foot PT boat during a training exercise out of Melville, Rhode Island. The man in the foreground is handling an ammunition magazine for the piece.

Camouflaged PT-132, nicknamed "Little Lulu," served with Squadrons 7 and 21 in the Southwest Pacific. Although it was an early Elco 80-foot boat, having been launched August 28, 1942, by the time of this photograph, it had been updated to include 37 mm and 20 mm cannons on the foredeck, Mk. 50 5-inch rocket launchers, drop racks rather than torpedo tubes, and a 1945-style radar mast.

PT-132 was painted in a variation of the Measure 31 camouflage scheme. From this angle, the canvas awning above the bridge is clearly visible, as is the aft 40 mm mount. In the foreground is the Mk. 50 5-inch rocket launcher of another PT. Like scores of other PT boats, PT-132 was stripped and burned at Samar in November 1945.

PT-166, here just prior to launching, was one of a squadron of 80-foot Elco boats painted in this experimental "Zebra" scheme, intended to confuse the enemy as to the type and bearing of the boat. A squadron of Higgins 78-foot boats was painted in a similar scheme. PT-166 was destroyed by USAAF B-25 bombers in a friendly-fire incident off New Georgia in the Solomon Islands on July 20, 1943.

The Elco boats painted in the Zebra scheme were sent to the Pacific, while the similarly painted Higgins boats went to the Mediterranean. Virtually every part of the boat was covered in the camouflage scheme.

The port quarter of PT-169 shows off the Zebra camouflage application on the rear of the vessel. The camouflage even extended over the canvas covers for the 20 mm cannon and .50-caliber machine guns.

Owing in part to the complexity of the paint scheme, and the difficulty of applying and maintaining the scheme, there were no further PT boats so painted beyond the initial two squadrons.

The fleet oiler USS *Atascosa* (AO-66; formerly the SS *Esso Columbia*) takes advantage of its light-load condition to transport zebra-stripe camouflage-painted Elco PT boats as deck cargo from the Norfolk Navy Yard, in Portsmouth, Virginia, on March 14, 1943. The boats are stored on supports both forward of and to the rear of the bridge. *National Archives*

A dusting of snow has fallen on 80-foot Elco PT boats of Squadron 9, secured three abreast above the main deck of SS *White Plains* in New York in December 1942. These boats were about to be shipped to Panama. Note the radar installation with the fabric cover on the boat to the left rear, PT-155. Next to it is PT-152. In less than a year, in 1943, this boat would be operating in New Guinea and sporting artwork of a vulture on the front of the charthouse. *National Archives*

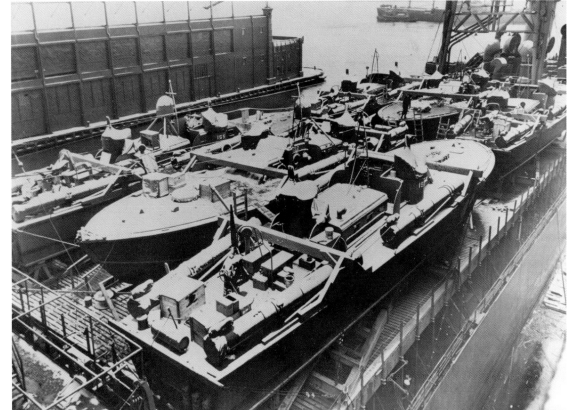

PT-196 was factory-painted with a shark's-mouth bow and a wavy camouflage pattern on the hull sides. At the tip of the bow, a fairlead with a navigation light has been mounted, and visible above the windshield is a wind and spray deflector.

For part of its life, PT-196 was also equipped with an experimental auxiliary fuel tank. Extending from the stern, the tank was designed to be discarded once emptied. Ultimately, PT-196 served with Squadron 12 at New Britain Island, New Guinea.

The second contracted class of Elco 80-foot boats was the PT-314 to PT-367 series. The lead boat was PT-314, the keel of which was laid on December 11, 1942, and it was completed on March 11, 1943. Construction of the class was completed on July 27, 1943. The hull and basic structure of these boats were the same as the previous class, with minor changes. Among them, the spray shield was removed from around the engine room hatch, and the former simple hatch gave way to a taller combination hatch/ventilator.

Resting in the Elco boathouse, from left to right, are PTs 314, 317, and 316, all nearing completion. All three have their early-type masts retracted, and torpedo tubes, armament, rigging, and foredeck life raft are yet to be installed.

"Green Beast," as PT-333 was known, exhibits the first standardized radar mast model used on 80-foot Elcos. This style of mast was introduced on the Elco PT-486–563-class boats but was later retrofitted to some earlier boats, including PT-333. The mast incorporated a radome at the top and could be lowered in order to provide clearance beneath docks, boathouses, bridges, and other overhanging obstructions.

PTs 362 through 367 were assembled by Harbor Boat Building in Terminal Island, California, using kits produced by Elco's Bayonne plant. They were identical in design to the PT-314 to 361 boats.

Another of the 80-foot Elco boats assembled by Harbor Boat Building, PT-364, is shown tied up in the Southwest Pacific. The boat, which served with Squadron 18, is painted in a Measure 31 camouflage scheme. Among PT-364's armament are a pair of Mk. 50 rocket launchers and an M4 37 mm cannon on the bow.

Mk. 50 rocket launchers were designed to swing out for firing, as shown here, or inboard for storing or reloading. At the bottom of the mount is the electrical ignition cable, used to connect the firing circuits of the launcher with controls in the bridge. The rocket tubes were manually elevated at the mount but were fixed in azimuth, with the direction of the boat controlling traverse.

The crew of an unidentified Elco 80-foot PT boat has gathered behind the port Mk. 50 5-inch rocket launcher of their boat. A variety of 5-inch spin-stabilized rockets were produced for these launchers, providing a range of between 2,500 and 10,000 yards. This gave the PT a salvo equal to that of a destroyer broadside. The torpedoes have been decorated with painted shark faces.

At the top of the Mk. 50 launcher, seen here from the rear loaded and in the firing position, is the elevation crank. In the center foreground is the front of a torpedo in the the forward starboard drop rack.

Although this boat is unidentified, it is known that five boats of Squadron 24 were fitted with 4.5-inch barrage rocket racks such as those in front of the charthouse on this boat. These racks could fire a volley of twenty-four rockets in four seconds. Adding to the bombardment capabilities, a mortar is mounted in front of the starboard rack. Two depth charges are secured behind the smoke generator on the stern.

PT-380 was part of the PT-372–383 class, all of which were completed between August 3 and August 28, 1943. It was photographed shortly after completion off Brooklyn, New York. Just ahead to the port of the charthouse is visible a 20 mm Oerlikon autocannon. PT-380 was assigned to Squadron 28 in the Southwest Pacific.

While the previous photo was taken at the beginning of PT-380's service life, this image was captured near the end. PT-380, by then nicknamed the "Hellion," has been hoisted aboard a tender preparatory to decommissioning.

Elco PT-487 speeds along in this factory-captured photo taken around its completion date of January 10, 1944. It was assigned to Squadron 4, the torpedo boat training unit at Melville, Rhode Island, until that unit was decommissioned and the boat was placed out of service on January 28, 1946. On August 27 of the same year, it was reclassified as Small Boat C105336.

In this later view, PT-487 boasts a retracted 1945-type radar mast, Mk. 50 rocket launchers with protective covers, and other late-war armaments and fixtures. This photo was probably taken on one of the Great Lakes during a bond tour in October 1945.

Completed on November 2, 1943, PT-558 was a member of the PT-486 to PT-563 class. It was one of the few boats fitted with the Elco Thunderbolt gun mount. Assigned to Squadron 29 in the Mediterranean, during the night of June 14–15, 1944, it took part in the sinking of two German corvettes near Genoa, Italy. Later, it was returned to the US for use as a training boat.

Various means of mounting the 37 mm Oldsmobile autocannon on PT boat bows were utilized, including this interesting mount. The gun shield is field fabricated, as evidenced by the torch marks on the sides. The 37 mm magazine is full.

A Mk. 6 depth charge is shown in a type C rack (or, as they were called in the technical manual, a "release track"). A two-piece release cable connecting the outboard side of the rack with the release lever at the center of the inboard side of the rack holds the depth charge in place. When that lever is pulled up, the depth charge is released.

The 40 mm gun crew of PT-562 demonstrates the loading and aiming process. The loader with headphones is ready to drop a four-round ammunition clip into the gun's automatic loader, while at right a man passes another clip from the 40 mm ready ammunition locker. The boat was assigned to Squadron 29 from 1943, and was off Nice, France, when this photo was taken. She was transferred to the Soviet Union on April 7, 1945, and upon return under the provisions of Lend-Lease, she was scuttled in the Barents Sea in 1956.

The Elco Thunderbolt was an experimental quadruple 20 mm gun mount. The power-driven mount was armed with four 20 mm Oerlikon guns and magazines, with a seat and controls for a gunner, and could deliver devastating gunfire. Four boats assigned to Squadron 29 were equipped with these mounts. Here, PTs 558, 557, and 559 with their Thunderbolt systems, along with other PT boats, transit a stateside canal.

The Thunderbolt was originally envisioned as having six .50-caliber machine guns augmented by a pair of 20 mm autocannons. Through development, the number of 20 mm guns increased, and the number of .50-caliber machine guns decreased, until by January 1943 the .50-caliber machine guns were eliminated altogether. This early model Thunderbolt was installed on PT-160 for testing in late 1942.

PT-579 was completed on March 1, 1945, and assigned to Squadron 39, which was commissioned March 6, 1945. Part of the Elco PT-565–624 class, the boat served at Samar in the Philippines from July 1945 to the end of the war, never seeing action.

PT-579 was painted in the Measure 31, Design 20L four-color camouflage scheme. The scheme was composed of Outside Green 2 and Outside Green 3, with black on the vertical surfaces and Deck Green on the decks.

Typical of late–World War II PT boats, PT-579 was armed with a suite of 20 mm, 37 mm, 40 mm, and .50-caliber guns, and 5-inch rocket launchers. Supporting the barrel of the 40 mm gun here is the limit stop (also called the pipe railstop), a frame designed to prevent the gunners from shooting up the cabin, bridge, torpedo tubes, or mast while tracking enemy targets.

PT-594, an Elco 80-foot motor torpedo boat, was launched and completed during April 1945. Assigned to Motor Torpedo Boat Squadron 40, it was shipped to Samar, Philippine Islands, in the summer of 1945 but did not see combat. This boat bore a nickname, "States Happy," which was painted on a placard attached to the roof of the charthouse. Although the placard shows up in other photos of the boat, it is only faintly visible here, on the port side of the life raft on the charthouse roof. This boat had a 37 mm cannon and a 20 mm cannon (both of which have their covers on) on the foredeck and a 40 mm Bofors gun on the fantail. Note the small boat, with camouflage paint applied, stored upside down on the day cabin.

Various members of the crew take their positions aboard PT-596, "Hell Razor," in a stateside port. The boat was completed on May 10, 1945, and assigned to Squadron 40 in the Philippines. Although it arrived in theater, it saw no action and was placed out of service on December 21, 1945. The boat's nickname is on a plaque adjacent to the life raft.

The Mk. 50 rocket launchers of PT-588 are in their inboard stored position. The nearly new boat's 37 mm automatic cannon, with its 30-round magazine on top, is visible near the bow. The 37 mm was highly useful during barge-busting operations.

Resting on the foredeck of PT-588 is the anchor. Also visible are several hull vents along the edge of the deck, the various ammunition lockers on the foredeck, and the life raft stowed atop the charthouse.

PT-588 was commissioned on April 10, 1945. As seen from a dockside, a dinghy was stowed atop the day cabin. Also visible are the details of the roll-off torpedo system as well as the radar mast.

As seen in this nearly overhead view of the bridge area of PT-588, the once very clean lines of the Elco 80-foot design, as exemplified by PT-103 (seen on page 92), have during the course of the war become cluttered with an array of antennas, weapons, ammunition stowage, and survival equipment.

Six mufflers protrude from the stern of PT-588. The Elco exhaust system featured cutouts. Normally, the exhaust gases were routed through the mufflers, but when maximum performance was required, the butterfly valves of the cutouts were opened via a linkage in the engine compartment, allowing the exhaust gases to flow unrestricted out of the rear of the boat. The result was an increase in horsepower, at the expense of losing any chance of going undetected.

Stanchions support steel rope lifelines around the side of the deck of PT-588. On the fantail is mounted a 40 mm Bofors gun, shown here in the stowed position, its muzzle resting atop the limit stop. Just forward of the limit stop is a 40 mm ammunition locker atop the engine room hatch.

After World War II, the US military found itself with vast amounts of military hardware, much of it in the far-flung corners of the world. The PTs, not only excess to the Navy's needs but also of wooden construction and thus difficult to preserve, were among the excess. Large numbers of the boats were stripped of engines and armament and burned, as seen here.

Dozens of PTs, some veterans, some nearly new, were torched at Samar, Philippines, on November 9, 1945.

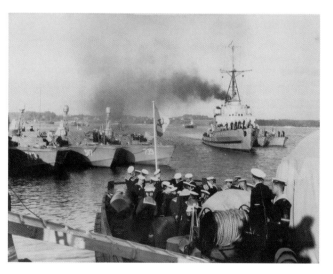

The terms of Lend-Lease required that the military equipment, if not lost in combat, either be returned or paid for. The Soviet Union, which disputed their bill, returned several PT boats in July 1955, including these. These vessels are part of about a dozen PT boats turned over in Kiel, Germany. Most were subsequently stripped and scuttled by the US.

Manufactured by the Electric Launch Company, Bayonne, New Jersey, PT-617 was an 80-foot Elco boat launched on July 28, 1945, and completed on September 21 of that year. The boat was sold to a private bidder in October 1947, later serving as a yacht and utility boat. PT Boats Inc. bought PT-617 in 1979 and restored it to its World War II configuration. It is on display at Battleship Cove, Fall River, Massachusetts. *Photo by author*

As seen from the foredeck, two 37 mm ammunition lockers are to the front of PT-617's charthouse. The boat's number is painted on the front of the bridge. A spotlight is on the port side of the bridge, and a radome on a foldable mast is to the rear of the bridge. On the starboard side are a 60 mm mortar and a twin .50-caliber machine gun turret. *Photo by author*

The front of the charthouse is viewed from another angle, showing how the bridge is offset to the port side of the centerline. A life raft is atop the charthouse, and a torpedo tube is to each side of the charthouse. *Photo by author*

The 60 mm mortar, useful for shelling Japanese positions while the PT boat was operating as a gunboat, is shown nestled on its foundation. *Photo by author*

The mast, atop of which rests the radome, is mounted on two large hinges on the front of the day cabin roof and has an A-frame brace on the rear. When necessary to clear overhanging obstacles, it was possible to undo the brace and lower the mast and radome to lay flat on the day cabin's roof. *Photo by author*

A partial view of PT-617's bridge includes the helm, the instrument panel, the throttle controls with the Elco logo embossed on the cover, and, above the throttle controls, a compass. *Photo by author*

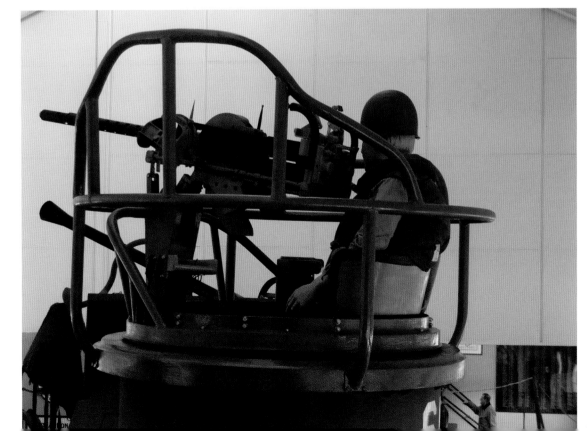

A mannequin in helmet and life jacket is poised between the twin .50-caliber machine guns in the starboard turret of PT-617. The depression rails were attached to the fixed part of the turret and physically prevented the guns from being aimed and fired at structures on the boat. The tubular rails on the movable part of the turret were for bracing the pedestal supporting the machine guns. *Photo by author*

The stern of PT-617 is displayed. The diagonal wooden planking of the hull is particularly visible in the red-painted area below the boat's waterline. The mufflers may be replicas, since they vary from the type usually seen in wartime photos and lack the linkages for the butterfly valves. *Photo by author*